AUDIO
ACCESS
INCLUDED

SINGER'S EDITION

Disney PRINCESS SONGBOOK

Includes 8 Songs
With Warm-Ups and
Vocal Instruction

To access audio visit:
www.halleonard.com/mylibrary

Enter Code
1292-0238-7820-1274

ISBN 978-1-4950-5324-5

Walt Disney Music Company
Wonderland Music Company, Inc.

DISTRIBUTED BY

HAL•LEONARD®
CORPORATION
7777 W. BLUEMOUND RD. P.O. BOX 13819 MILWAUKEE, WI 53213

In Australia Contact:
Hal Leonard Australia Pty. Ltd.
4 Lentara Court
Cheltenham, Victoria, 3192 Australia
Email: ausadmin@halleonard.com.au

Visit Hal Leonard Online at
www.halleonard.com

Text by Danielle Aldach

Vocals: Sarah Richardson

Piano: J. Mark Baker

Recording Engineer: Ric Probst

The vocal warm-up tracks feature a demonstration of the exercise, then two repetitions by the piano. Listen the first time, then sing along with the piano.

4   Almost There

12   A Dream Is a Wish Your Heart Makes

18   I Wonder

22   Part of Your World

30   Reflection

34   Something There

39   When Will My Life Begin?

44   Where Do I Go from Here

Almost There

The Princess and the Frog

Tiana

Head down to New Orleans for a lesson with Tiana. She is the best princess to teach you breath support. **Breath support** is a vocal technique used to sustain a healthy sound for a long period of time when singing. This first exercise will help you to use your diaphragm. The diaphragm is a flat dome-shaped muscle located just below your lungs. It plays an important role in breathing. Place one hand on your stomach, and feel it expand as you inhale. You should feel it push downward and out just a little with each consonant. In the second exercise, use part of Tiana's song to the evening star to practice taking a nice full breath before singing.

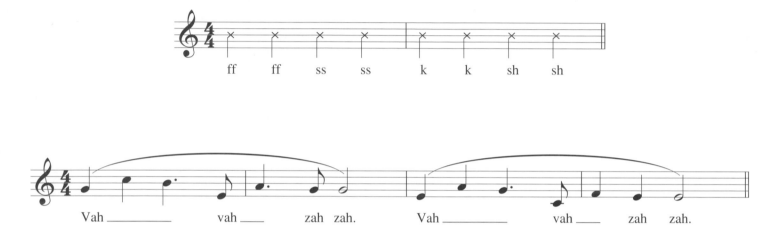

Almost There
from Walt Disney's THE PRINCESS AND THE FROG

Music and Lyrics by
Randy Newman

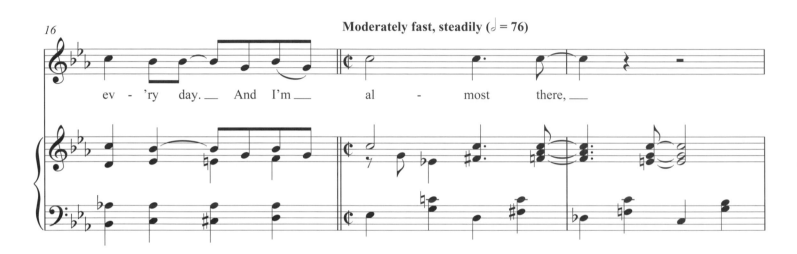

Trials _____ and trib - u - la - tions, I've had ___ my share. ___

___ There ain't noth - ing gon - na stop me now ___ 'cause I'm ___

al - most there. ___

I re - mem - ber Dad - dy told ___

me   fair - y tales can come true, ____

but you got - ta make 'em hap - pen; it all de-pends on ____ you. ____

_____   So I work ___ real hard ___ each and ev - 'ry day. ___   Now

things for sure ___ are go - ing my way. ___   Just ___ do - ing

what I do, ___ look out, boys, ___ I'm ___ com - in' through. ___ And I'm ___

al - most there, ___ I'm al - most there. _

___ Peo - ple gon - na come here from ev - 'ry - where, _ and I'm

al - most there, ___ I'm al - most there. _

There've been trials and trib - u - la - tions. You know I've___ had ___ my

share. But I've climbed a moun - tain, I've crossed a riv - er, and I'm

al - most there. _____ I'm al - most there. _

I'm ___ al - most there. _____

A Dream Is a Wish Your Heart Makes

Cinderella

Cinderella

We find Cinderella in the ballroom to practice singing chromatic notes. A musical scale is made up of 12 notes, each a half step apart. **Chromatic** notes are those that do not appear in the key. In a piece of music, these are also referred to as **accidentals**. First, let's practice descending and ascending chromatics. In the second exercise, use part of Cinderella's theme to practice accurate pitches. Use a piano or the recording to listen first, then sing along.

A Dream Is a Wish Your Heart Makes

from Walt Disney's CINDERELLA

Words and Music by Mack David,
Al Hoffman and Jerry Livingston

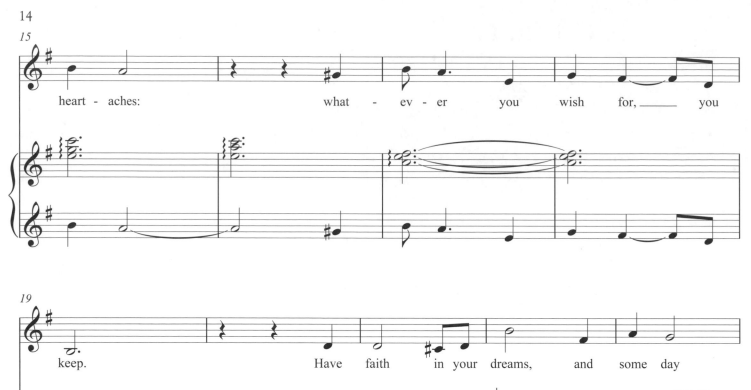

heart - aches: what - ev - er you wish for, _____ you

keep. Have faith in your dreams, and some day

your rain - bow will come smil - ing through. No mat - ter

how your heart is griev - ing, if you keep on be - liev - ing, the dream _____

that you wish will come true.

cresc. poco a poco

accel.

Slightly faster (♩. = c. 52)

mf

A dream is a wish your

ff   *mf*

heart makes _____ when you're fast a - sleep.

In dreams you will lose your heart - aches: what -

ev - er you wish for, _____ you keep. Have

faith in your dreams, and some day your

rain - bow will come smil - ing through. No mat - ter

how your heart is griev - ing, if you keep on be - liev - ing, the

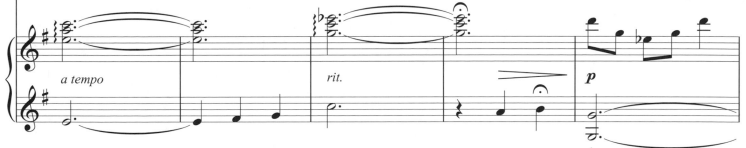

dream _____ that you wish will come true. _____

I Wonder

Sleeping Beauty

Aurora

Let's go for a walk in the woods with Aurora for a lesson in intervals. An **interval** is the distance between two notes. This distance can be large or small. In the first exercise, we will practice small intervals. In the second exercise, we will practice large intervals. Use a piano or the recording to listen first, then sing along.

I Wonder
from Walt Disney's SLEEPING BEAUTY

Words by Winston Hibler and Ted Sears
Music by George Bruns
Adapted from a Theme by Tchaikovsky

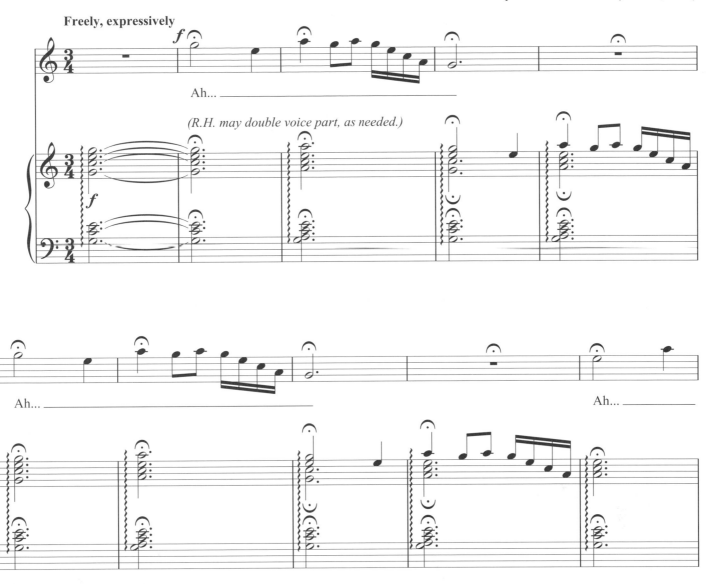

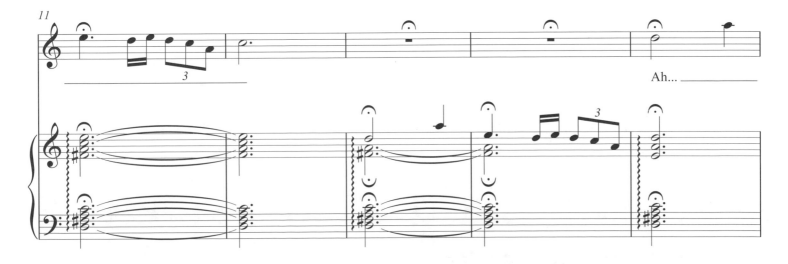

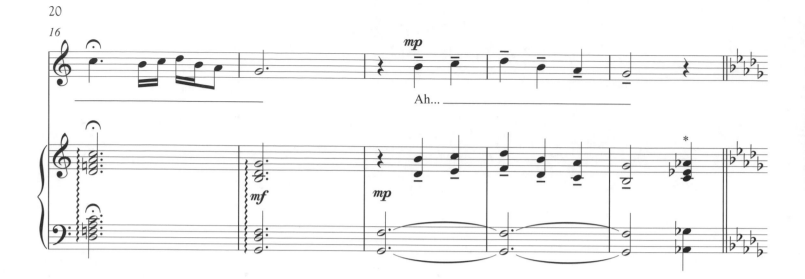

* For a shorter version, begin here.

A gay lit - tle love mel - o - dy? _____ I

won - der, _____ I won - der _____ If my heart keeps

sing - ing, will my song go wing - ing to some - one _____ Who'll

find me _____ And bring back a love song to me?

Part of Your World

The Little Mermaid

Ariel

Go for a swim in the sea with Ariel to practice singing legato. **Legato** is the Italian word for smooth. Notes in succession should be sung in one connected breath with no space in between. Use Ariel's theme, first ascending, and then descending, to practice singing smoothly.

Part of Your World
from Walt Disney's THE LITTLE MERMAID

Music by Alan Menken
Lyrics by Howard Ashman

Look at this trove, ___ treas-ures un-told. ___ How man-y won-ders can

one cav-ern hold? Look-ing a-round ___ here you'd think, ___ sure, she's got

ev-'ry-thing. ___ I've got gad-gets and giz-mos a-

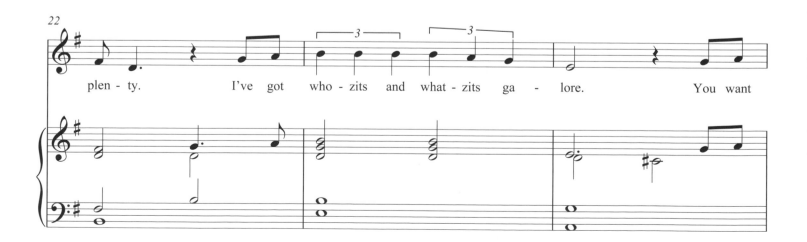

plen-ty. I've got who-zits and what-zits ga-lore. You want

thing-a-ma-bobs, I've got twen-ty. But who cares? No big

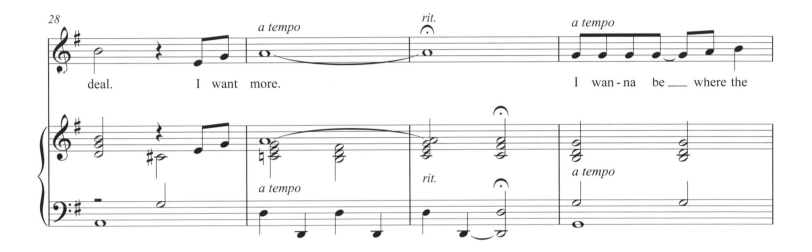

deal. I want more. I wan-na be ___ where the

peo-ple are. I wan-na see, ___ wan-na see 'em danc-in',

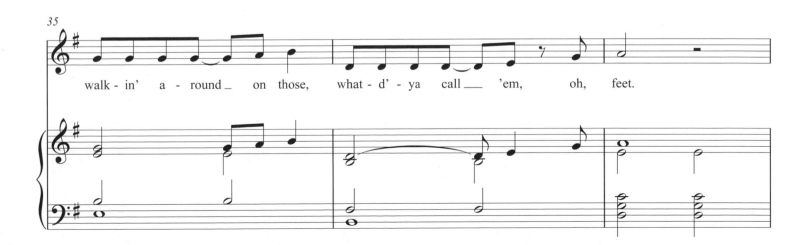

walk-in' a-round ___ on those, what-d'-ya call ___ 'em, oh, feet.

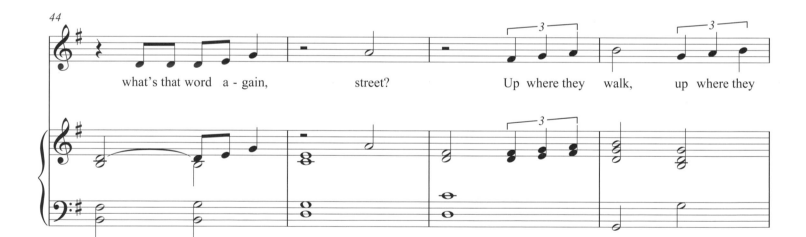

free, wish I could be part of that world._____ What would I

give if I could live out-ta these wa-ters? What would I

pay to spend a day warm on the sand? Bet-cha on

land they un-der-stand. Bet they don't re-pri-mand__ their daugh-

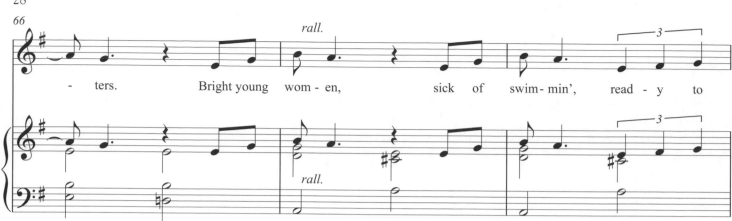

When's_ it my turn? Would-n't I love, love to ex-plore that shore up a-

bove,_____ out of the sea. Wish I could

be part of that world._____

Reflection

Mulan

Mulan

Time to practice in the training fields with Mulan. Here we will learn to sing using dynamics. **Dynamics** are indications of the levels of sound, loud or soft, in a piece of music. In this first exercise, practice singing one whole note at a time. Begin softly, grow louder, and then come back down to soft. In the second exercise, use the dynamics given throughout the melody.

Reflection
from Walt Disney Pictures' MULAN

Music by Matthew Wilder
Lyrics by David Zippel

be my-self, I would break my fam - 'ly's heart.

Who is that girl I see

star - ing straight back at me? Why is my re - flec - tion some - one

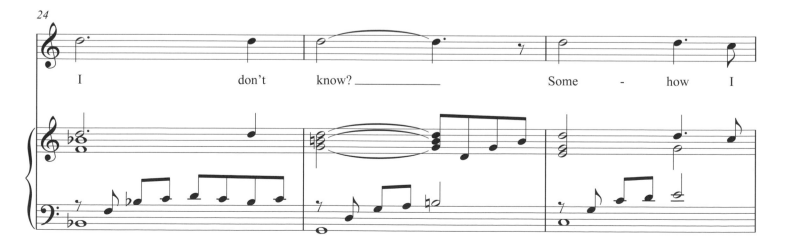

I don't know? Some - how I

can - not _____ hide who I am, though I've tried.

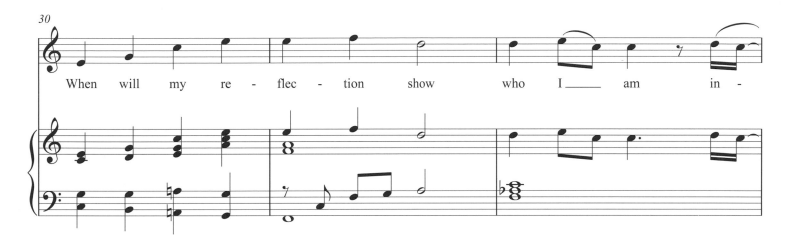

When will my re - flec - tion show who I _____ am in -

- side? _____ When will my re - flec - tion show who I _____ am in -

side? _____

Something There

Beauty and the Beast

Belle

Belle is on the staircase with the Beast practicing arpeggios. **Arpeggios** are the tones of a chord played in succession. In the next two exercises, make sure each note is sung on pitch – and remember to sing legato!

Something There

from Walt Disney's BEAUTY AND THE BEAST

Music by Alan Menken
Lyrics by Howard Ashman

why I did-n't see it there be-fore.

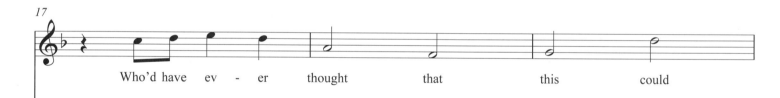

New, _____ and a bit a - larm - ing.

Who'd have ev - er thought that this could

be? _____ True _____

that he's no Prince Charm - ing, but there's some - thing

in him that I sim - ply did - n't see.

Well, who'd have thought? Well, who'd have

known? And who'd have guessed we'd come to - geth - er on our

own? Wait and see... a few days more. There may be

some-thing there that was-n't there be - fore. There may be

some-thing there that was-n't there be - fore.

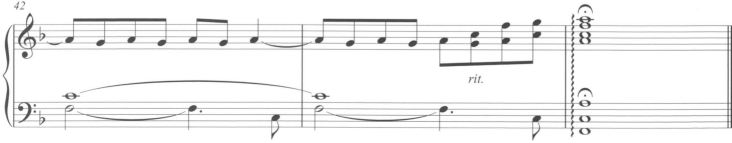

rit.

When Will My Life Begin?

Tangled

Rapunzel

Rapunzel is the best teacher for rhythm. Rhythm is how notes are counted – long and short lengths. The next two exercises are from Rapunzel's song. Clap and speak each rhythm to practice for "When Will My Life Begin." Use the audio recording if you need to.

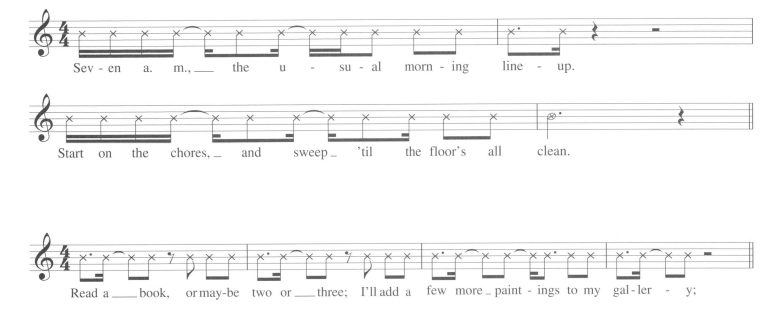

Sev - en a. m., ___ the u - su - al morn - ing line - up.

Start on the chores, _ and sweep _ 'til the floor's all clean.

Read a ___ book, or may-be two or ___ three; I'll add a few more _ paint - ings to my gal - ler - y;

When Will My Life Begin?

from Walt Disney Pictures' TANGLED

Music by Alan Menken
Lyrics by Glenn Slater

Moderately fast Rock (♩ = 104)

Sev - en a. m., the u - su - al morn - ing line - up.
Then af - ter lunch, it's puz - zles, and darts and bak - ing...

Start on the chores, and sweep 'til the floor's all clean.
pa - pier mâ - ché, a bit of bal - let and chess...

Pol - ish and wax, do laun - dry, and mop, and shine up. Sweep a -
pot - ter - y and ven - tril - o - quy, can - dle - mak - ing... then I'll

gain, and ___ by then it's, ___ like, sev - en ___ fif - teen. And so I'll
stretch, may - be sketch, take ___ a climb, sew ___ a dress. And I'll re -

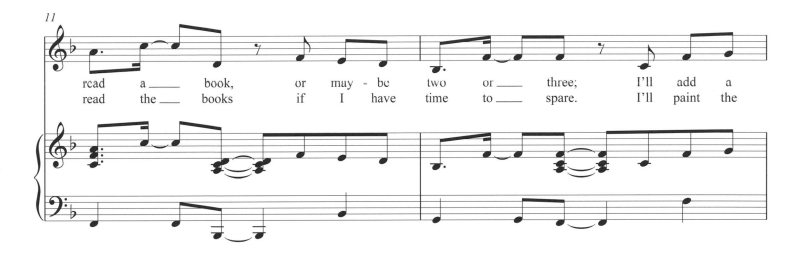

read a ___ book, or may - be two or ___ three; I'll add a
read the ___ books if I have time to ___ spare. I'll paint the

few more ___ paint - ings to my gal - ler - y; I'll play gui -
walls some ___ more; ___ I'm sure there's room some - where. And then I'll

tar, and ___ knit, and cook, and ba - sic - 'ly ___ just won - der,
brush, and ___ brush and brush, and brush my ___ hair, ___ stuck in the

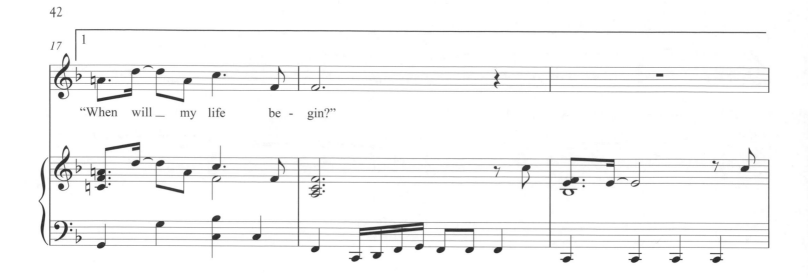

"When will__ my life be - gin?"

same place__ I've al - ways__ been, and I'll keep won - d'ring__ and won - d'ring__ and

won - d'ring__ and won - d'ring, "When will__ my life be - gin?"

rit.

44

Where Do I Go from Here
Pocahontas II: Journey to the New World

Pocahontas

Pocahontas will help you learn phrasing. A **phrase** in music is a complete thought. Think of it like a sentence. The singer expresses the rise and fall of the notes in a complete musical sentence. In the first exercise, use the theme from Pocahontas to apply this musical concept. In the second exercise, practice using the theme from "Where Do I Go from Here" to prepare for the whole song.

Where Do I Go from Here
from Walt Disney's POCAHONTAS II: JOURNEY TO A NEW WORLD

Music by Larry Grossman
Words by Marty Panzer

they sur-vive. ___ When snow's so deep, the bears all sleep to
hard to see, ___ it winds and bends, but where it ends de -

keep them-selves a-live. They do ___ what they
pends on on-ly me. In my heart ___ I

must for now and trust in their plan.
don't feel part of so much I've known.

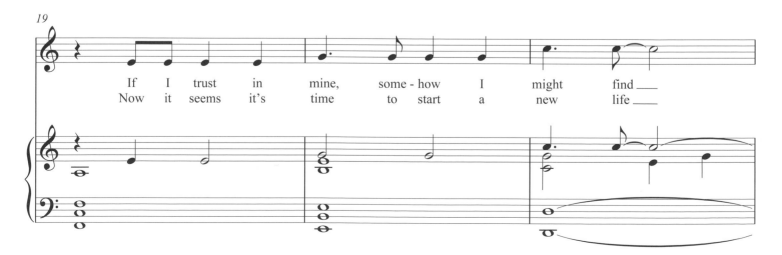

If I trust in mine, some-how I might find ___
Now it seems it's time to start a new life ___

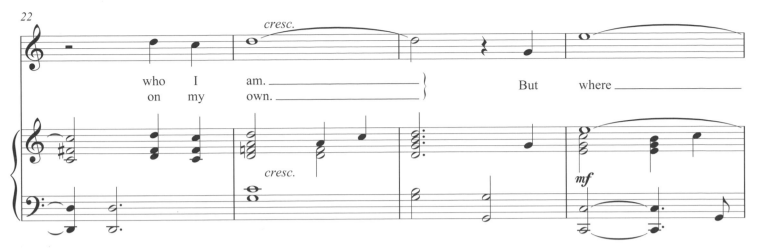

who I am. _____ But where _____
on my own. _____

_____ do I go from here? So man - y voic - es

ring - ing in ____ my ear. Which is the voice _____ that

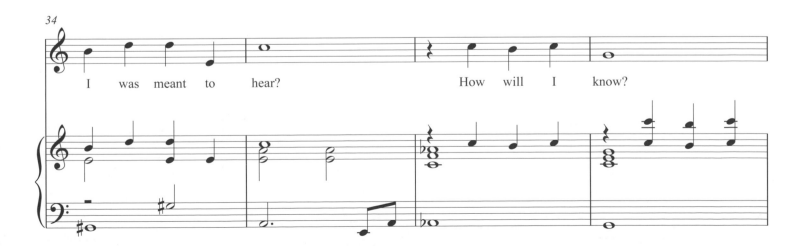

I was meant to hear? How will I know?

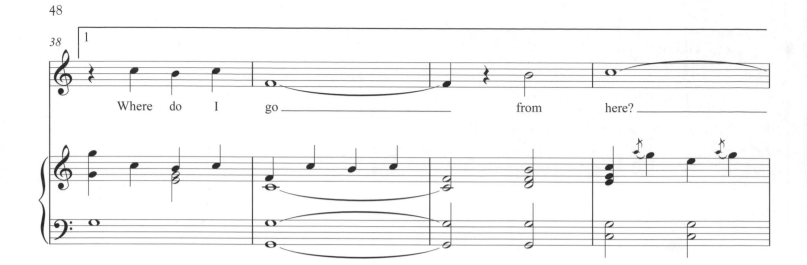

Where do I go _____ from here? _____

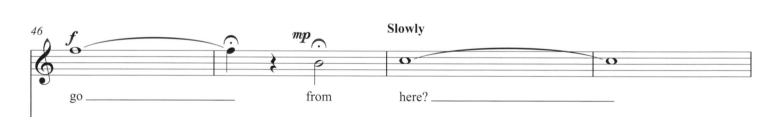

My Where do I

Slowly

go _____ from here? _____

dim. e rit.

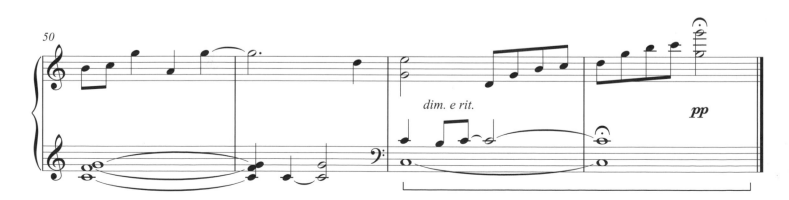